# Love Unaccommodated

# Love Unaccommodated

*Poems by Genevieve DiNatale*

CW Books

Published by CW Books
P.O. Box 541106
Cincinnati, OH 45254-1106

ISBN: 9781625493439

Poetry Editor: Kevin Walzer
Business Editor: Lori Jareo
Visit us on the web at: readcwbooks.com

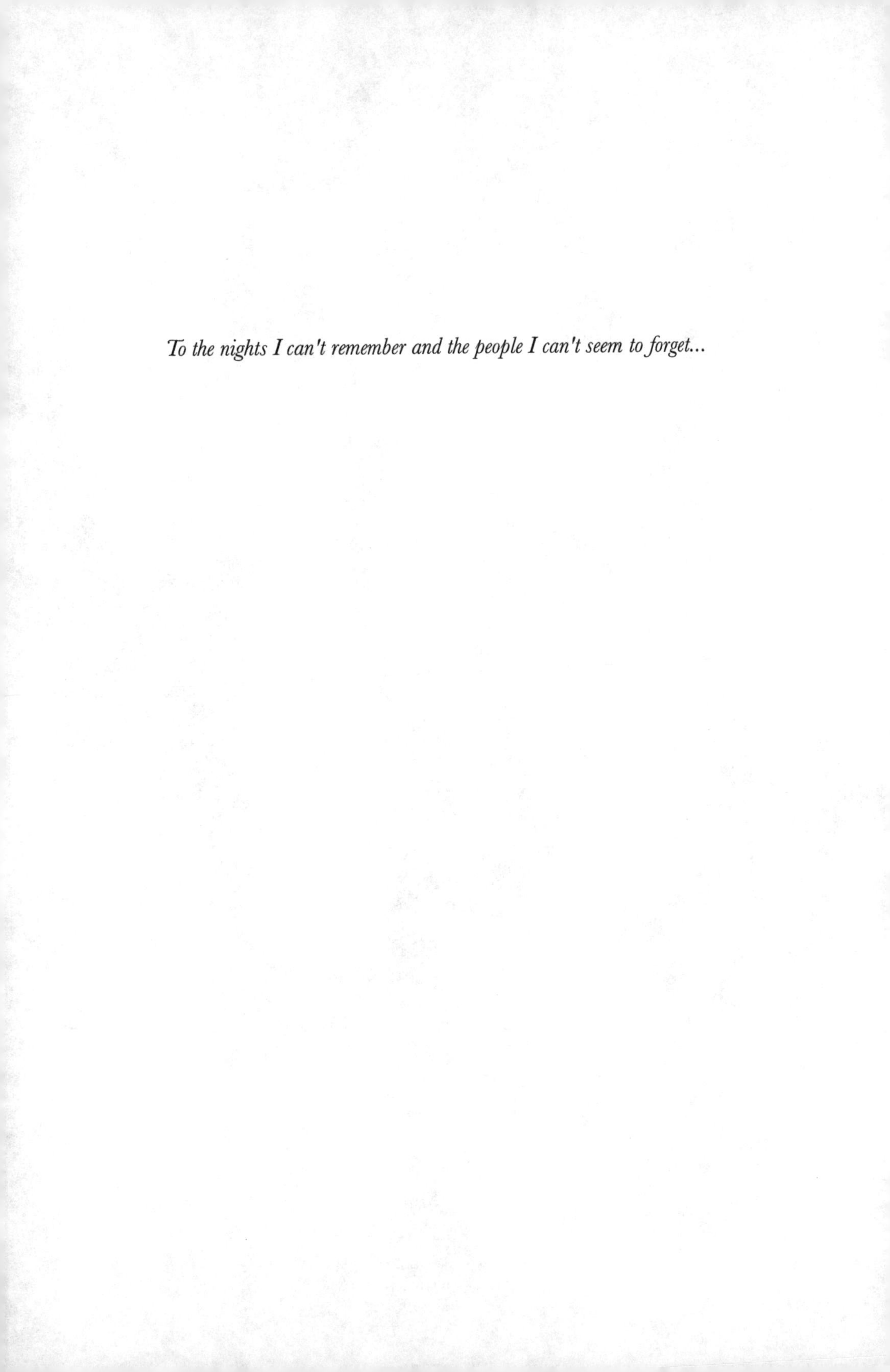

*To the nights I can't remember and the people I can't seem to forget...*

I would like to thank the editors of the following publications for previously publishing some of the poems that appear in this book: *The Santa Fe Writers Project, Penultimate Peanut Magazine,* and *The Voices Project.*

# Table of Contents

# My Mother's Garden

She wanted a normal life
Though all her appliances were broken
And all she had to show for it
Was a sash of satin laid carefully across the floor
With the neighbor boy's footprints in it

After her husband left
They laughed when she tended her garden:

*Hemerocallis,*
*Lilium convallium,*
*Dederunt hyacinthum,*
*Rhododendron ferrugineum*

She knew all their Latin names
Yet, no one noticed anything but the disorder that was attributed to her

And her dead words

## The Caterpillar On Your Door

The uninvited
Rejected
Ignored
Caterpillar on your door
Startles your grip

Green & supple
From a puddle
She's prey to your forgotten touch

Perhaps she's waiting for wings
To take flight

Or for her yellow stripes to harden
Into a brown cloak-cocoon
To depend upon

Yet, repulsed by the vulnerability
Of her metamorphosis
You brush past
Mouth closed
Teeth gnashed

## Your 15th Date

Differentiated by broken remembrance
The last petal — fallen from grace

He said,

'The world is full of people who haven't died yet'*[1]

The world's variation
Is breeds - is spectrum - is autonomy
And our greatest sin
Everything we are guilty of
Is skin

Discretion - our discrimination
And the melting petal

Is in our hands

So much to say between two entities
A known universe

Yet to be defined
Today

It's all there

And the satellites that fill your mind and mine

Are simply bouncing off each other

Glancing across the table

The variance between two souls

---

1 (with special thanks to Franz Wright's poem 'On Earth' for concept)

Two days
Burnt by the same

Sun

And the other one

The moon

That you wish for in light

The separation between the quality of you

And what you envision of another

Is simply miscommunication

Bouncing off one thought into another

Conversation

Sad souls

Sipping on plastic straws

In a forgotten place

That still exists

## A Date With A Finnish Physicist

All the world's complexities fell upon him
Like leaves from a gigantic tree

Twisted and disheveled he took a seat
Before an anonymous girl in a country foreign to him
And parroted back
Everything she wanted to hear
In her own language

But it wasn't enough
The twirling smoke signals
Of his windblown hair
Wasn't enough

The Biblical tear-stained tower
Crumpled by her side in agony
Wasn't enough

The look in his eyes
That reached to the beginning of time
Wasn't enough
To convince her

That no matter the length

No matter when the leaves brush the hollow ground with their brittle spines

No matter when the smoke clears into the empty sky

Or when the last rain falls
On his closed eyes

She didn't want to fall
This time

## The Prom

I

both accepted & rejected
the nominated prom queen
took to the sticky gym floor
and danced alone
her blue sparkly dress fluttered in the stuffy air
as the latest pop songs filled her ears until she screamed with false delight

she was once a chubby child
seated at the edge of a pool
reading an autobiography of Ben Franklin
as her parents looked on in awe

now she's a nominated prom queen
without a date
dancing to Celine Dion as her AP history teacher looks on in disgust

II

pupil specks
ash long as cigarettes
lines of cocaine
on the back of a cd in the bathroom

it's prom night in Bolton
the lights went out hours ago
the police are on patrol

and the nominated prom queen
sits on a loveseat
watching "Lock, Stock & Two Smoking Barrels"
during the overdose

## III

all that remained were the tracks in Mary's lawn
it was a week before prom
and he didn't make it
collapsed on the bathroom floor
I cried knowing
neither would I
empty circles & cold shoulders
all signs point to nowhere
nevertheless, the crumpled up car outside the police department stood as a stark reminder
of proms past

## IV

all he never told me
came back to me from someone else

I tried to make something of myself
Snow White on Halloween
his girlfriend
a prom queen
the teacher I always wanted
but never had

transfixed by becoming
spurned by negative reinforcement from a formative time
I morphed from one thing to another
and then continued to change through the dissatisfaction

## V

two weeks after the prom
and the bubble party
he opened his hand

try this
my father's a doctor
he annunciated in a false-falsetto
it was Bethany's second cousin
from far away
where I drifted off to
after the movie
how long (ago) was it?
she asked

## Cancer Stricken Love

We both flinched
My heart wasn't even visible
Yet you watched as I thumbed through CDs
At Rody's Records
And took an extra long walk to your car
Because I wanted to stay awhile

We talked about the part of Dante's Inferno
I hadn't read yet
Laughed about the circles of hell
While smoke trails ran about your head

I was so young
We were separated by miles, generations, contracts & contacts
Nevertheless, you took me to chemotherapy
Before smoking a cigarette in the parking lot of the hospital
I never understood why & I'll never forgot

The day you collapsed on the kitchen floor &
Begged me for a glass of water
That I wasn't prepared to get
I honestly didn't know how to do it
I watched you writhe in pain on the blue tile
In your skinny jeans

And now that you're long gone, I recall how
We watched a Monarch butterfly pass
A large rock in the woods
In Savannah, Georgia, while I was in college

You were the only man unoffended by my sensitivities
Untouched by the things you watched me see
Like beautiful, transient insects
Passing by

## "Forever Burned"

How we met is still a mystery
He invited me through his window
Long ago

I twisted the crank and pushed out the cobweb covered screen
Scraped my belly across dead flies so I could
Pull myself into his dusty scene
Complete with mattress on the floor
A Ziplock bag full of brownies
And a poster of Van Gogh's earliest work
"Skull of a Skeleton with Burning Cigarette"

All he wanted was a taste of this morning's toothpaste
A crumb on his lip to lick off — a smudge
To pluck and stick

All he wanted
Was entry
Intrigue

Take the window
Take me
Steal your way in & I'll make you
Regret

But...
I agreed to transcend a barrier
So transparent it proved
You'd have love to lose

I turned the crank & forced it open
Pushed the screen out with my palm
While he waited
For me to come crashing

Were a dearth of opportunities the precursor to this?
Was I misled by a head of windswept curls and a kind gesture?
Is that all it took?
Because I can't remember.
Perhaps a nice statement
Led me
Like a cat-burglar quietly folding her hand around a familiar door
Was I the one who stalked her way into a one-sided love story?

Was I the one who burned the candle on the plywood?
Did I stick it there with its own wax?
Did I enter his eyes to watch it burn?

If only I knew

## See You Later

You let the time pass
Like a train hurtling by
You left me standing there
Drooling on my shoes

If I touch it, I'll probably die
And if I remain standing, I'll tremble

Either way.

## “Dear Mr. Sandman”

Dash across the water lilies
Tread through the clover
Tell me it isn’t over
Take me & don’t let go
Until we’re too old

## The Indiscernible Fruit Of Your Desire

So what am I?
The indiscernible fruit of your desire
A response to a repetitive question

Identity subsumed by availability
Lightning veins of historic impulse
Left hanging from a branch
Broken by a passing thunderstorm
That only struck twice

So what am I?
A fleeting thought
Shrouded by secrecy
Met with the resistance of longevity
After an instant of touch
Only to be forgotten

So what am I?
A moment of time left counting

A meadow of flowers in full bloom
For you to plow though

Or a vase to be crushed and replaced
Filled with blank, empty space

So interchangeable you'll never notice

Or am I the echo of your primal screams
That come hurtling back years later
When you least expect it

## Shiloh

Otherworldly orbs danced in the hands of another
His passenger
Unassuming, she grasped each and held it

"Take a look"

Triangulated
By planetary distance
Was the endless gap
That separated our love
And in her nubile palm was a man

Named Shiloh

He rubbed his legs against her
Like a sick, inconsolable child
Tossed about
In his own
Existential abyss

A gasp escaped my lips
As a door opened

On the train to Leominster

Our serious kiss
Of tangerine mist
Was piss in her palm

## Missed you on the Interstate

Like speeding bullets
Cars shot past

My head swirled

I had a

*
F
*
L
*
A
*
S
*
H
*
B
*
A
*
C
*
K
*

I miss you so much

## To A Younger Man

When you've finally reached the point where
You've had too many bad experiences
To react normally
*Call me*

## Rude Awakening

So there I was
Seated in my car
In front of a building
I didn't want to enter
Talking to a man
Hundreds of miles away
Through my Bluetooth

Consoling vibration

Detached & connecting
Over aluminum alloy
Carbon graphite
Copper
&
Gold

So that's what I've been told

II

## Winter Psalm

She waited
*Then...*
Walked along a winter psalm
Without whispered words

## Tomorrow into Oblivion (The 6th Grade)

All that fell through the sky shined

Then it shriveled up and died

On tomorrow's doorstep

Little beads of oblivion

Puffed silver dust

And the tear of the sentient one

Fell in its place

And...

No one could tell the difference

But he cried

And in his stained shirt

Raised his hand

And asked about tomorrow

# After the Breakdown

She rises in smiles
And like a flashlight through an asylum door
Makes her daily rotation
With such delicacy, that
Finding the exact turning point is itself a science

Meanwhile the electrodes burn your skull
&
Pulsating through your brain
Are the little lasers of false light
That we call hope

But with your last wits about what's left
You return to your seat
To watch the rest of Ellen

## Happily Unmarried

Geriatric and rocking just feet away
From her deathbed, the unwidowed-widow
Rattled off a story, crumpled to her side
With paper-thin skin that splits with
Every movement
The ants slowly crawl toward her across the floorboards
Imagined rattling is just the minute-hand and
Her wrinkled old hands fail to entice
Another's grip
Like the old red lipstick sitting on her dresser with
A Bayer aspirin stuck in it
She rocks and rocks and makes small talk
As the flies spin 'round her head
(As if she's already dead)

# My Mind

An intractable place
A small, leather briefcase
Full of cloths, receipts
Used tissue and deceit

Free from containment
It flies from within

Loses air as it spins

Angles of sin
In the end

## Fired

In the back of my mind
Linger reaper's reeds
Tossed about in the breeze

Don't ask me when I'm gone
Where I'm going to
Swollen formaldehyde lips
Beg the question

## *KILL THIS*

Which morality is in question?
That of the race or that placed upon
A woman's place
Without valor, without honor

But with grace

Men gone to war
Their valor - their morality

Then me...
In line at CVS
Somewhere in Waltham, Massachusetts

Waiting for Plan B

He would barely stand beside me

But where is my valor?
In the line?
Or with Lawrence Kohlberg
Who took his life at sea

Legs shaking at the clinic
Alone
But to myself I am known
And I know that I have honor
With or without an unborn daughter

With or without sleepless nights
Medical bills and pants that are too tight
To take seriously
Don't question my morality
Because
You won't call me a hero

Indecision sent men to Vietnam
And his decision sent a child into my arms

And who is to say that my choice
Is not moral?

Ask Carol Gilligan.

Ask the 12-year-old incest victim
Walking through closed doors
Through chants of "whore"
Why doesn't she care anymore?

Ask Donald Trump's children
From multiple women
What is the moral of his decision?

To speak for an incest victim?

He told me to come over late one night

All I had to give was torn, tossed and twisted
Lost and because I am not gifted, I am given
The gift of life — never to be your wife
Because my pants were too tight

Because we met at night

By myself at the clinic
We never even kissed
KILL THIS.

## "Immaculate reception"

Neon flashes
The fish at Bethany's house
Their smoke tails curled about her face

Her mother's brown curls
Looked dashing in the blue light
Of an infomercial
Some 20 years ago
In Massachusetts

"Immaculate reception"
I said of the cross
Hanging above her television

Take your shoes off
Move in
Remove your skin
Let it all hang out
On a rusty fence in Marlborough

In the 8th grade Bethany told me
That my clothes didn't match
That I grasped my right breast
Rather than my heart
During the Pledge of Allegiance

Bethany also knew Chloe
Who knew Paul

And one day in homeroom
Chloe asked me
If I smelt pot on her
I said, "What's that?"

She said weed
And she smoked that
By the river this morning
After she had sex

Large-breasted and blond

On the bathroom floor
Flayed and poor evermore

Neon flashes in my mind

## The Dove

"I'm only here for the night," said the dove
On the windowsill
Of my old apartment in Brooklyn

It's 2013

They say dust
Is what remains
Of a star

"I'm like a magpie at the beach," he added
This is your life
Your illusion

"Perhaps even your delusion," he chuckled
And before I could reply

He was gone

## The Simian Man

The Simian man wiled away in a tower
Just a blip that cast a long shadow
Hundreds of feet below

And with an insanity both pure and true
He pulled himself together
Rattled off some numbers
Grabbed a rope
And the handle of an AK-47

Bloodstained handprints on the sidewalk
Bloodstained shirts on the classroom floor
Trembling underneath
America's last heartbeat

Yet through the insignificance
His long shadow made its way
To the tip of children's shoes
To the storefront
And to you…

# The Bleeding Nomad

The bleeding nomad
Fell to his knees
In the fanciest part of town
And screamed

His hair, matted and torn
His face, washed out and worn
There's no indication that he ever looked good
&
That's something he clearly understood
You could tell by the way
He gripped his face
As he let it all out
That life really made its way to him